~A BINGO BOOK~

Ancient Greece Bingo Book

COMPLETE BINGO GAME IN A BOOK

Written By Rebecca Stark

ISBN 978-0-87386-477-0

Educational Books 'n' Bingo

Printed in the U.S.A.

ANCIENT GREECE BINGO
Directions

INCLUDED:

List of Terms

Templates for Additional Terms and Clues

2 Clues per Term

30 Unique Bingo Cards

Markers

1. **Either cut apart the book or make copies of ALL the sheets. You might want to make an extra copy of the clue sheets to use for introduction and review. Keep the sheets in an envelope for easy reuse.**

2. Cut apart the call cards with terms and clues.

3. Pass out one bingo card per student. There are enough for a class of 30.

4. Pass out markers. You may cut apart the markers included in this book or use any other small items of your choice.

5. Decide whether or not you will require the entire card to be filled. Requiring the entire card to be filled provides a better review. However, if you have a short time to fill, you may prefer to have them do the just the border or some other format. Tell the class before you begin what is required.

6. There are 50 topics. Read the list before you begin. If there are any topics that have not been covered in class, you may want to read to the students the topic and clues before you begin.

7. There is a blank space in the middle of each card. You can instruct the students to use it as a free space or you can write in answers to cover topics not included. Of course, in this case you would create your own clues. (Templates provided.)

8. Shuffle the cards and place them in a pile. Two or three clues are provided for each topic. If you plan to play the game with the same group more than once, you might want to choose a different clue for each game. If not, you may choose to use more than one clue.

9. Be sure to keep the cards you have used for the present game in a separate pile. When a student calls, "Bingo," he or she will have to verify that the correct answers are on his or her card AND that the markers were placed in response to the proper questions. Pull out the cards that are on the student's card keeping them in the order they were used in the game. Read each clue as it was given and ask the student to identify the correct answer from his or her card.

10. If the student has the correct answers on the card AND has shown that they were marked in response to the *correct questions,* then that student is the winner and the game is over. If the student does not have the correct answers on the card OR he or she marked the answers in response to *the wrong questions,* then the game continues until there is a proper winner.

11. If you want to play again, reshuffle the cards and begin again.

Have Fun!

TERMS INCLUDED

ACHILLES

ACROPOLIS

AGORA

ALEXANDER THE GREAT

APHRODITE

APOLLO

ARES

ARETé

ARISTOTLE

ARTEMIS

ATHENE (ATHENA)

ATHENS

CHAOS

CHITONS

CITY-STATE

COLUMNS

CYCLOPS

DELIAN LEAGUE

DEMETER

DEMOSTHENES

DIONYSUS

ECHO

HADES

HELIOS

HERA

HERACLES

HERMES

HEPHAESTUS

HERODOTUS

HIPPOCRATES

HOMER

JASON

MINOANS

MINOTAUR

OLYMPIC GAMES

ORACLE

PEGASUS

PELOPONNESIAN WARS

PERICLES

PERSIAN WARS

PLATO

PLAYWRIGHTS

POSEIDON

PROMETHEUS

SOCRATES

SOLON

SOPHISTS

TITANS

TROJAN WAR

ZEUS

Additional Terms

Choose as many additional terms as you would like and write them in the squares. Repeat each as desired.
Cut out the squares and randomly distribute them to the class.
Instruct the students to place their square on the center space of their card.

Ancient Greece Bingo

Clues for
Additional Terms

Write three clues for each of your additional terms.

_____ 1. 2. 3.	_____ 1. 2. 3.
_____ 1. 2. 3.	_____ 1. 2. 3.
_____ 1. 2. 3.	_____ 1. 2. 3.

©

ACHILLES
1. This mythological hero of the Trojan War was invulnerable on all parts of his body except for his heel.
2. He was the central character and the greatest warrior of Homer's *Iliad.*
3. Thetis, his mother, tried to make him immortal by dipping him in the river Styx.

ACROPOLIS
1. Literally, it means "high city."
2. It was located on the highest ground and contained the most important municipal and religious buildings.
3. The Parthenon was located on the one in Athens.

AGORA
1. It was the marketplace and most important meeting place of the ancient Greek city-states.
2. Men looking for jobs as well as employers looking for workers gathered there.
3. The name for the anxiety disorder which causes people to fear being in public places, especially places where crowds gather, is based on this Greek word.

ALEXANDER THE GREAT
1. He became king of Macedon when his father, Philip II of Macedon, died.
2. By the time of is death in 323 BCE, he had conquered most of the world known to the ancient Greeks.
3. He conquered the Persian Empire and annexed it to Macedonia.

APHRODITE
1. She was the goddess of beauty and love.
2. Her equivalent in Roman mythology is Venus.
3. In some versions of the myth she married the smith Hephaestus, who foolishly made her a magic girdle that made her irresistible.

APOLLO
1. This god of light and of the sun was also god of poetry and music, especially the lyre. He guided the choir of the Muses.
2. His name was the same in Roman mythology.
3. He was very handsome; therefore, we sometimes refer to a very handsome man by his name.

ARES
1. He was the god of savage warfare in Greek mythology.
2. His equivalent in Roman mythology is Mars.
3. Deimos, the god of terror, and Phobos, the god of fear, were his constant companions in war.

ARETÉ
1. It might be described as the condition of living up to one's full potential.
2. Synonyms might be "excellence" or "virtue."
3. Homer used the term to describe the strength and courage of the heroes.

ARISTOTLE
1. This Greek philosopher was a student of Plato and a teacher of Alexander the Great.
2. He established a school in Athens c. 335 BCE. It was known as the Lyceum.
3. Some of his treatises include *Ares, Metaphysics, Politics, De Anima* (On the Soul) and *Poetics.*

ARTEMIS
1. She was the goddess of wild animals, the hunt and childbirth.
2. Her equivalent in Roman mythology is Diana.
3. This goddess was the daughter of Leto and Zeus and the twin sister of Apollo.

Ancient Greece Bingo

ATHENE (Athena) 1. She was the goddess of wise counsel, war, the defense of towns, weaving, pottery and other crafts. 2. Her equivalent in Roman mythology is Minerva. 3. Her temple, built in the 5th century BCE on the Athenian Acropolis, is called the Parthenon.	**ATHENS** 1. Poseidon and Athene vied for dominion of this city-state. 2. This city-state is sometimes called the "Cradle of Democracy." 3. This city-state became an Empire under Pericles, who ruled from c. 460 to 429 BCE. It dominated the other city-states.
CHAOS 1. In Greek mythology it was the original state of existence from which the first gods appeared. 2. Some myths describe it as a void in which things existed in a confused and amorphous shape. 3. Although the myths vary, some say that Gaia, or Earth, was born from this void.	**CHITONS** 1. These tunics were the main item of clothing for men. 2. These large squares of cloth were held in place by pins at the shoulders and a belt round the waist. 3. Women wore similar items of clothing, but theirs went to their ankles.
CITY-STATE 1. The Greek name for it was *polis.* 2. The most important ones were Athens, Sparta, Corinth, Delphi, and Thebes. 3. Although the people from the different ones were all Greek, they had different customs and beliefs.	**COLUMNS** 1. Of the three styles found in ancient Greece, Doric was the simplest. Doric ones were plain but powerful looking. 2. Ionic ones were fluted and had tall shafts, making them look slender. 3. Corinthian ones were the most decorative.
CYCLOPS (Cyclopes, plural) 1. In Greek mythology it is a member of a primordial race of giants, each with one eye in the middle of its forehead. 2. In Homer's epic poem the *Odyssey,* the ___ Polyphemus captures the Greek hero Odysseus. 3. These one-eyed giants were metal workers and blacksmiths; they gave Zeus the gift of thunder and lightning.	**DELIAN LEAGUE** 1. It was an association of about 150 Greek city-states under the leadership of Athens. 2. It was a military organization founded in the fifth century as an alliance against the Persian Empire and led by Athens. 3. This alliance developed into an Athenian Empire under Pericles.
DEMETER 1. She was the earth goddess who brought forth the grains and other fruits of the earth. 2. Her Roman equivalent is Ceres. 3. The earth brought forth no grain when she wandered the Earth searching for her daughter Persephone, who had been abducted by Hades.	**DEMOSTHENES** 1. He was an Athenian statesman and orator. 2. He is considered the greatest of all ancient Greek orators. 3. It is said that as a boy this great orator had a speech impediment and that he practiced to improve his locution.

Ancient Greece Bingo

DIONYSUS	ECHO
1. He was the god of wine, vegetation, pleasure and festivity. 2. His equivalent in Roman mythology is Bacchus. 3. He was born from the thigh of Zeus after his mortal mother Semele was destroyed by Zeus's lightning.	1. She was a mountain nymph who loved her own voice. 2. She fell in love with Narcissus, but her love was unrequited. 3. Hera punished her by having her always repeat the voice of another.
HADES	**HELIOS**
1. Brother to Zeus and Poseidon, he was the god of the nether world, or world of the dead. 2. His equivalent in Roman mythology is Pluto. 3. This referred to the Underworld itself as well as to the god who ruled it. The river Styx came between it and the earth.	1. He personified the sun and was the son of Hyperion and Theia. 2. In later times he was identified with Apollo, the god of light. 3. When his son Phaëton attempted to drive his chariot, he lost control and set the earth on fire.
HERA	**HERACLES**
1. As the wife of Zeus, she was the queen of the Olympian deities. 2. Her equivalent in Roman mythology is Juno. 2. She was the goddess of marriage and birth.	1. Son of the Zeus and the mortal Alcmene, this hero was extremely strong. 2. He was told by the oracle to perform twelve labors, or tasks. 3. His first labor was to kill the Nemean Lion.
HERMES	**HEPHAESTUS**
1. He was the messenger of the gods and was the god of roads, travel, hospitality, merchants and commerce. 2. As messenger of the gods, he guided the souls of the dead to Charon, the ferryman who took them to Hades. 2. Like his equivalent in Roman mythology, Mercury, he wore winged sandals.	1. This god of fire was the patron of all craftsmen, especially those working with metals. 2. His Roman equivalent is Vulcan. 3. He caused Hera to be imprisoned in a magic throne which he had fashioned, but he released her when Aphrodite became his bride.
HERODOTUS	**HIPPOCRATES**
1. He lived in the fifth century BCE and is regarded as the "Father of History." 2. He is best known for writing The *Histories,* considered the first work of history in Western literature. 3. His great work, *The Histories,* chronicles the rise of the Persian Empire and its war with the Greek city-states. Ancient Greece Bingo	1. He was an ancient Greek physician during the Age of Pericles. 2. He is sometimes called the "Father of Medicine." 3. It is believed that he wrote the oath regarding the ethics of practicing medicine typically taken by physicians.

HOMER
1. He is believed by many to be the author of two epic poems, but some scholars think the name is fictitious.
2. He is credited with having written the *Iliad,* which tells the story of the siege of Troy.
3. He is credited with having written the *Odyssey*, which tells of the wanderings of Odysseus.

JASON
1. He was the heroic leader of the Argonauts.
2. His ship was the *Argo*.
3. His quest was to find the Golden Fleece.

MINOANS
1. They lived on the island of Crete during the Bronze Age.
2. They are also called Myceneans after the best-preserved of their cities.
3. One of their popular sports was bull-jumping; both men and women participated.

MINOTAUR
1. This creature was part man and part bull.
2. This creature lived at the center of the Labyrinth, a maze-like construction built by Daedalus for King Minos of Crete.
3. This creature was killed by the hero Theseus.

OLYMPIC GAMES
1. They were a series of athletic competitions held among the city-states of ancient Greece.
2. They began in 776 BCE in Olympia and continued until 393 CE.
3. Prizes were in the form of olive wreaths, palm branches and woolen ribbons.

ORACLE
1. The one at the temple of Delphi was the most important.
2. The one at Delphi was consulted before wars and other major undertakings.
3. The ancient Greeks believed the gods could give them advice by speaking through one.

PEGASUS
1. According to some versions of the myth, this winged horse was the son of Poseidon and sprung from the neck of Medusa when she was killed by the hero Perseus.
2. Bellerophon tamed him.
3. Zeus honored this winged horse by making him a constellation.

PELOPONNESIAN WARS
1. These were a series of conflicts in which Athens and its empire fought against the Peloponnesian League, which was led by Sparta.
2. These conflicts took place from 431 to 404 BCE.
3. The Greek historian Thucydides, who lived from c. 460 BCE to c. 395 BCE, is known for his history of these conflicts.

PERICLES
1. He led Athens during its Golden Age.
2. He turned the Delian League into the Athenian Empire.
3. He fostered democracy, promoted arts and literature, and started a building project that included the Parthenon.

PERSIAN WARS
1. An important battle of this war was the Battle of Marathon, which occurred in 490 BCE.
2. Darius I was king during the first invasion of this conflict. Xerxes was king during the second.
3. The Battle of Salamis was an important naval battle of these conflicts.

PLATO
1. He was a student of Socrates and a mentor of Aristotle.
2. He founded the Academy in Athens, the first institution of higher learning in the western world.
3. Many of his dialogues feature Socrates.

PLAYWRIGHTS
1. Aeschylus, Sophocles and Euripides were this. They were all tragedians.
2. Aristophanes was one. He is sometimes called the "Father of Comedy."
3. In addition to tragedies and comedies, some wrote satyr plays, which were based on mythology.

POSEIDON
1. Brother to Zeus and Hades, he was the god of the sea.
2. His Roman equivalent is Neptune.
3. His symbols include dolphins, tridents, and three-pronged fish spears.

PROMETHEUS
1. According to one legend, he stole the sacred fire from the gods and gave it to man.
2. Zeus punished him by having him chained to a rock in the Caucasus where his liver was picked at daily by an eagle (or vulture).
3. Heracles eventually saved him from his eternal punishment by killing the bird who picked at his liver and freeing him.

SOCRATES
1. His most famous pupil was Plato. Most of our knowledge about him comes from Plato.
2. He was convicted of undermining the state religion and corrupting the youth of Athens. He was sentenced to death by hemlock in 399 BCE.
3. His "method" involved asking probing questions in a give-and-take manner to lead to the truth.

SOLON
1. This Athenian statesman, lawmaker and lyric poet lived from c. 638 BCE to 558 BCE. He was one of the Seven Sages.
2. He tried to legislate against political, economic and moral decline in Athens.
3. Although not a democrat, Cleisthenes later used his reforms as the basis for forming a democracy in c. 508 BCE.

SOPHISTS
1. They were a group of teachers of philosophy and rhetoric, the art of speaking effectively.
2. Protagoras, who lived from c. 490 to 420 BCE, is usually regarded as the first of these pre-Socratic philosophers.
3. It came to denote general wisdom, especially in politics and ethics. The Seven Sages of 7th and 6th centuries BCE were called this.

TITANS
1. Also known as the elder gods, the first generation of these deities ruled the earth until the Olympians overthrew them.
2. Cronus and Rhea led the first generation of these gods; they were the parents of Zeus and the other Olympian gods and goddesses.
3. Some second-generation ones included Atlas, Prometheus, Eos, and Selene.

TROJAN WAR
1. In mythology it was waged against the city of Troy by the Achaeans.
2. Its mythical cause was the abduction of Helen from her husband Menelaus by Paris of Troy.
3. The *Iliad* was an epic poem about this 10-year war; it was set during its ninth year.

ZEUS
1. He was the supreme rule of the Olympian gods.
2. His Roman equivalent is Jupiter.
3. His main attribute was the thunderbolt; he controlled thunder, lightning and rain.

Ancient Greece Bingo

© Barbara M. Peller

Ancient Greece Bingo

Persian Wars	Achilles	Apollo	Hera	Delian League
Alexander the Great	Acropolis	Solon	Minoans	Olympic Games
Aphrodite	Titans		Oracle	Trojan War
Zeus	Columns	Socrates	Hippocrates	Minotaur
Pegasus	Demosthenes	Helios	Sophists	Hephaestus

Ancient Greece Bingo

Zeus	Aphrodite	Herodotus	Poseidon	Hades
Minotaur	Chitons	Aristotle	Columns	Homer
Athens	Demosthenes		Cyclops	Socrates
Pericles	Playwrights	Titans	Plato	Delian League
Olympic Games	Solon	Helios	Alexander the Great	Sophists

© Barbara M. Peller

Ancient Greece Bingo

Demosthenes	Socrates	Chitons	Hippocrates	Aphrodite
Minoans	Acropolis	Athene	Achilles	Heracles
Columns	Solon		Homer	Agora
Titans	Athens	Pegasus	Pericles	Herodotus
Sophists	Alexander the Great	Helios	Plato	Hades

Ancient Greece Bingo: Card No. 3

© Barbara M. Peller

Ancient Greece
Bingo

Ancient Greece Bingo

Titans	Homer	Apollo	Alexander the Great	Hades
Hermes	Areté	Achilles	Poseidon	Aphrodite
Oracle	Pericles		Hephaestus	Hera
Socrates	Demeter	Solon	Helios	Aristotle
Artemis	Olympic Games	Ares	Sophists	Trojan War

Ancient Greece Bingo

Olympic Games	Delian League	Columns	Aristotle	Alexander the Great
Hermes	Socrates	Athene	Cyclops	Acropolis
Apollo	Trojan War		Minoans	Dionysus
Hephaestus	Hades	Persian Wars	Plato	Chaos
Chitons	Helios	Aphrodite	Titans	Oracle

Ancient Greece Bingo: Card No. 5

© Barbara M. Peller

Ancient Greece Bingo

Agora	Homer	Herodotus	Hades	Trojan War
Hippocrates	Columns	Chaos	Achilles	Aphrodite
Poseidon	Artemis		Areté	Cyclops
Helios	Pegasus	Plato	Ares	Apollo
Minotaur	Aristotle	Persian Wars	Oracle	Demeter

Ancient Greece Bingo

Persian Wars	Homer	Dionysus	Minoans	Chitons
Minotaur	Hades	Demosthenes	Acropolis	Hermes
Herodotus	Hera		Cyclops	Areté
Titans	Pericles	Athene	Zeus	Athens
Helios	Alexander the Great	Plato	Ares	Agora

Ancient Greece Bingo

Ancient Greece Bingo

Oracle	Homer	City-State	Hippocrates	Areté
Hermes	Apollo	Poseidon	Trojan War	Aristotle
Demeter	Peloponnesian Wars		Hades	Delian League
Sophists	Titans	Zeus	Artemis	Pericles
Solon	Helios	Ares	Columns	Minotaur

Ancient Greece Bingo: Card No. 8

Ancient Greece Bingo

Cyclops	Chitons	Demosthenes	Demeter	Alexander the Great
Artemis	Hades	Oracle	Columns	Homer
Heracles	Persian Wars		Acropolis	City-State
Chaos	Delian League	Pegasus	Minoans	Dionysus
Pericles	Plato	Athene	Zeus	Hephaestus

Ancient Greece Bingo

Zeus	Hippocrates	Areté	Poseidon	Demeter
Trojan War	Aristotle	Achilles	Acropolis	Hades
Peloponnesian Wars	Homer		Hera	Athens
Pegasus	Hephaestus	Chaos	Plato	Heracles
Athene	Minotaur	Herodotus	Olympic Games	Oracle

Ancient Greece Bingo

Agora	Homer	Columns	Chaos	Minotaur
City-State	Heracles	Minoans	Cyclops	Achilles
Hermes	Hades		Herodotus	Demosthenes
Athene	Aphrodite	Plato	Alexander the Great	Zeus
Artemis	Helios	Persian Wars	Ares	Chitons

Ancient Greece Bingo: Card No. 11

© Barbara M. Peller

Ancient Greece Bingo

Ancient Greece Bingo

Chitons	Delian League	Heracles	Hippocrates	Cyclops
Demosthenes	Minotaur	Apollo	Ares	Acropolis
Persian Wars	Dionysus		Trojan War	Poseidon
Helios	Pericles	Hades	Zeus	Hermes
Homer	City-State	Peloponnesian Wars	Artemis	Aristotle

Ancient Greece Bingo: Card No. 12

Ancient Greece Bingo

Chaos	Delian League	Agora	Heracles	Trojan War
Apollo	City-State	Hades	Cyclops	Athens
Hippocrates	Aristotle		Demosthenes	Dionysus
Oracle	Plato	Areté	Peloponnesian Wars	Zeus
Helios	Hephaestus	Ares	Persian Wars	Minoans

Ancient Greece Bingo

Alexander the Great	Hades	Columns	Cyclops	Artemis
Aristotle	Persian Wars	Heracles	Acropolis	Homer
Chaos	Hera		Herodotus	Athene
Hephaestus	Plato	Peloponnesian Wars	Areté	Agora
Helios	Poseidon	Athens	Minotaur	Oracle

Ancient Greece Bingo

Minoans	Cyclops	Columns	Chitons	Hippocrates
Agora	Herodotus	Achilles	Apollo	Artemis
Trojan War	Persian Wars		Aphrodite	Homer
Helios	Heracles	City-State	Plato	Chaos
Minotaur	Pericles	Ares	Demeter	Demosthenes

Ancient Greece Bingo

Areté	Heracles	City-State	Demeter	Playwrights
Poseidon	Athens	Dionysus	Hermes	Hera
Chaos	Delian League		Trojan War	Demosthenes
Titans	Aristotle	Helios	Minoans	Zeus
Artemis	Prometheus	Ares	Pericles	Homer

Ancient Greece Bingo

Athene	Jason	Echo	Heracles	Alexander the Great
Minoans	Artemis	Plato	Hera	Dionysus
Cyclops	Oracle		Prometheus	City-State
Hephaestus	Minotaur	Zeus	Columns	Athens
Pegasus	Chaos	Chitons	Hippocrates	Delian League

Ancient Greece Bingo: Card No. 17

© Barbara M. Peller

Ancient Greece Bingo

Demeter	Peloponnesian Wars	Aristotle	Chaos	Poseidon
Homer	Athene	Pegasus	Trojan War	Artemis
Cyclops	Athens		Echo	Apollo
Delian League	Achilles	Plato	Zeus	Herodotus
Prometheus	Heracles	Columns	Jason	Agora

Ancient Greece Bingo

Trojan War	Agora	Heracles	City-State	Zeus
Minoans	Hippocrates	Homer	Chitons	Hera
Jason	Alexander the Great		Acropolis	Aphrodite
Herodotus	Prometheus	Pegasus	Pericles	Echo
Apollo	Playwrights	Minotaur	Oracle	Ares

Ancient Greece Bingo: Card No. 19

Ancient Greece Bingo

Ancient Greece Bingo

Peloponnesian Wars	Jason	Hippocrates	Heracles	Ares
Aristotle	Demosthenes	Hermes	Pegasus	Poseidon
Delian League	Dionysus		Titans	Achilles
Olympic Games	Solon	Sophists	Pericles	Prometheus
Socrates	Oracle	Playwrights	Zeus	Echo

Ancient Greece Bingo: Card No. 20

Ancient Greece Bingo

Minoans	Agora	Hermes	Heracles	Olympic Games
Delian League	Echo	Areté	City-State	Persian Wars
Athens	Minotaur		Jason	Columns
Pegasus	Chitons	Prometheus	Hephaestus	Oracle
Titans	Playwrights	Ares	Athene	Pericles

© Barbara M. Peller

Ancient Greece Bingo

Demeter	Herodotus	Echo	Apollo	Chaos
Poseidon	Hippocrates	Aphrodite	City-State	Acropolis
Aristotle	Hera		Persian Wars	Dionysus
Prometheus	Hephaestus	Pericles	Achilles	Alexander the Great
Playwrights	Athene	Jason	Athens	Hermes

Ancient Greece Bingo

Areté	Jason	Chitons	Apollo	Ares
Agora	Peloponnesian Wars	Minotaur	Minoans	Achilles
Herodotus	Chaos		Sophists	Persian Wars
Athens	Playwrights	Prometheus	Athene	Pericles
Olympic Games	Solon	Oracle	Pegasus	Echo

Ancient Greece Bingo: Card No. 23

© Barbara M. Peller

Ancient Greece Bingo

Areté	Peloponnesian Wars	Alexander the Great	Jason	City-State
Echo	Ares	Hermes	Poseidon	Persian Wars
Dionysus	Demeter		Chaos	Athens
Olympic Games	Sophists	Prometheus	Athene	Delian League
Socrates	Titans	Playwrights	Hippocrates	Solon

Ancient Greece Bingo

Titans	Hermes	Jason	Columns	Echo
Achilles	Delian League	Minoans	Areté	Acropolis
Hephaestus	City-State		Sophists	Prometheus
Aphrodite	Olympic Games	Solon	Playwrights	Hera
Ares	Alexander the Great	Aristotle	Artemis	Socrates

Ancient Greece Bingo

Echo	Jason	Herodotus	Poseidon	Demeter
Pegasus	Hippocrates	City-State	Peloponnesian Wars	Areté
Hephaestus	Sophists		Hera	Titans
Athene	Apollo	Olympic Games	Playwrights	Prometheus
Dionysus	Artemis	Columns	Solon	Socrates

Ancient Greece Bingo

Herodotus	Aristotle	Jason	Peloponnesian Wars	Demosthenes
Olympic Games	Sophists	Minoans	Prometheus	Acropolis
Plato	Solon		Playwrights	Titans
Demeter	Agora	Hermes	Socrates	Achilles
Artemis	Hera	Echo	Aphrodite	Dionysus

Ancient Greece Bingo

Ancient Greece	Peloponnesian Wars	Aphrodite	Jason	Areté
Demosthenes	Echo	Sophists	Poseidon	Hera
Solon	Athens		Dionysus	Pegasus
Zeus	Demeter	Minotaur	Playwrights	Prometheus
Apollo	Cyclops	Artemis	Socrates	Olympic Games

Ancient Greece Bingo: Card No. 28

Ancient Greece Bingo

Echo	Peloponnesian Wars	Demeter	Minoans	Cyclops
Energy	Pegasus	Hermes	Dionysus	Aphrodite
Hephaestus	Sophists		Acropolis	Jason
Demosthenes	Olympic Games	Hades	Playwrights	Prometheus
Areté	City-State	Socrates	Agora	Solon

Ancient Greece Bingo

Alexander the Great	Jason	Poseidon	Cyclops	Prometheus
Achilles	Peloponnesian Wars	Herodotus	Hera	Acropolis
Hephaestus	Chaos		Dionysus	Hermes
Socrates	Agora	Apollo	Playwrights	Sophists
Olympic Games	Chitons	Solon	Echo	Aphrodite

www.ingramcontent.com/pod-product-compliance
Lightning Source LLC
LaVergne TN
LVHW061337060426
835511LV00014B/1960